THE END OF Forever

Hope and Healing for the Hurting

Phyllis McColister

ISBN 979-8-88616-286-8 (paperback)
ISBN 979-8-88616-288-2 (hardcover)
ISBN 979-8-88616-287-5 (digital)

Christian Faith Publishing
832 Park Avenue
Meadville, PA 16335
www.christianfaithpublishing.com

Printed in the United States of America

ENDORSEMENTS

What an incredible read "The End of Forever" has been for our group. Your book spoke to all the women individually as well as collectively that led to overdue evaluations and discussions that then ushered us into a place of healing. Impressed with the Spiritual Shift sections, we were all challenged to evaluate our view. Thank you for your honesty and vulnerability because it led others to do the same. God continued blessings upon all you do as He pours you out for others to drink. You are a blessing.

Respectfully,
Pastor Ruth Mosley El Rio Lighthouse &
Founder of His Diamond Touch Corp

I have spent the past couple years on a journey of solitude and healing. "The End of Forever" played a major role in my healing. I highly recommend this book to women who are hurting or simply trying to figure things out.

Bree Graves

This book "The End of Forever " is beautifully written with wisdom, empathy, and a respect for Scripture. It will encourage, embolden, and empower women as they seek healing and restoration as they struggle through challenging marriages. I do appreciate the honesty that the author brings to this timely or (well needed) discussion on marriage, women and the church. I do recommend this book.

Minister Evadne Henry
Canada SDA Conference

Blessed *be* the God and Father of our Lord
Jesus Christ, the Father of mercies and God
of all comfort, who comforts us in all our
tribulation, that we may be able to comfort
those who are in any trouble, with the comfort
with which we ourselves are comforted by God.

—2 Corinthians 1:3, 4 NKJV

DEDICATION

There are few people that come into your life and give it such meaning and purpose as a child. My only child, Markeya Williams-Joeckel, entered my life and provided such beauty and purpose that I will always love her for it. She has never been a disappointment to me. I dedicate this book to her and all that she continues to be to me.

CONTENTS

Endorsements..v

A Note from the Author...xi

Part I: Introduction...1

Part II: The Beginning of Forever...5

Chapter 1: God's Ideal vs. Satan's Raw Deal..........................7

Chapter 2: Emotional Paralysis 11

Part III: The Threat of Forever 17

Chapter 3: Losing a Dream but Waking Up to Reality...........19

    Traveling toward Reality Road.......................................19

    Love and Goodbye 21

Chapter 4: Searching for Love in Human Hearts 26

Part IV: The Shame of Forever 31

Chapter 5: Broken Vows 33

    Necessary Separation 34

    Shame of Unfaithfulness..35

    Marital Accountability..36

Part V: The End of Forever 39

  Chapter 6: "Great Is Your Faithfulness" 41

    Earthly Failures 44

Part VI: The Hope of Forever 49

  Chapter 7: Misuse of Scripture 51

    Suffering Gone Too Far 51

    Misinterpretations of Grace 53

  Chapter 8: The Church's Response 55

  Chapter 9: Delightful Detours 60

    Hope in God..60

    There Should Be Some "Buts" in Your Life............61

    Comfort in Suffering..61

Part VII: The Eternal Forever....................................63

  Chapter 10: Bride of Christ 65

    Forever Restored...65

Exhibit A...67

Exhibit B...77

Are You in an Emotionally Destructive Relationship? 79

Exhibit C 87

Discussion Questions 89

Endnotes..103

A NOTE FROM THE AUTHOR

Hi, my name is Phyllis and I am a woman on a mission. A mission to reveal the love of Christ in His word. To reveal the relevancy and revolutionary power of His word that is demonstrative in the pages of this book. My voice is one that cries in the wilderness seeking to prepare a way to the Lord through the troubles that we face day-to-day. I cry tears of disappointment and dissatisfaction in the lost message of the relevancy of the love of Christ found in His word for every heartache in this life, especially emotional brokenness. We tend to go to church. Hear the word. Received the word gladly. But then the thorny ground and weeds of life experiences separate us from the rich blessing of being rooted, grounded and established in a love relationship with Christ. This book will lead you through one of the most painful experiences in life—divorce and/or separation. It will also provide you with step-by-step instructions on the practical application of God's Healing Plan (See Exhibits A & B).

My heart is broken by the lack of spiritual support and comfort from the church to minister the love of Christ and His word to this broken population. If God's word is not relevant to the death of marriages, then what do we do with the scripture that says, "My words are spirit and life" (John 6:63). Exhibit C is offered as loving guidance to the church as it ministers in a broken world to broken families.

What further breaks my heart is the well-meaning, but ill-advised Christians who lay heavier burdens on an already overloaded and overlooked soul-scrabbling Christians as they work their way through Christian divorces—the end of their "forever". Chapters 7

& 8 will encourage the body of Christ to represent Him in word and deed when ministering to its divorced/separated members.

If you are one of these soul-scrabbling Christians facing divorce or separation, then take the hand of this soul-scrabbling Christian. May we find the ever-present, everlasting, loving Savior with healing in His wings to shield us from the plans of the enemy to kill, steal and destroy our value and worth to the kingdom of God.

❦

PART I

Introduction

Forever is not supposed to end! What an utterly unbelievable, heart-wrenching, and life-altering experience. This book peeks into the pain and suffering of Christian women forced to face the end of marriage promises of forever that should only have been interrupted by death.

Conceivably, you were intrigued by the title of this book—*The End of Forever*. I was terrified and just as intrigued when the Holy Spirit led me to write a book on the subject of "Christian" divorce. Efforts to deny the damage of divorce in the church are still alive today and are responsible for short-circuiting the healing of God's people on every level. But even more damaging is the church's response to its divorced members.

We are socialized to believe that "Christian" divorce is an oxymoron. According to my friend, *Webster*, an *oxymoron* is a *figure of speech with apparently contradictory terms, a juxtapose in concepts with opposing meanings*. I can tell you from a tearful and broken heart that a "Christian" divorce is no "figure of speech" nor are the terms a mere juxtaposition but rather a concurrent reality that too often quarantines its wounded from self, others, and the healing power of God.

You may wonder why I chose to place Christian in quotes when referencing the subject of divorce in this book. Good question and I am so glad you are brave enough to ask. I encourage you to maintain the courage to keep asking those tough questions and expect satisfactory answers.

But I can promise you that God cares about the divorced. He does address this dreadful phenomenon shocking the Christian world today.

Join me on the journey to find healing and restoration even with a broken marriage. Yes, it is possible. Statistical evidence presented by the Barna Group, one of the leading research organizations in the United States, places the divorce rate among practicing Christians at 37 percent in 2019.[1]

There are approximately 205 million Christians in the United States, which means approximately 75,850,000 are divorced Christians.[2] We are not alone in this battle, and many soldiers need to hear the encouraging and empowering words of this book. You will find healing evidence that even with divorce on your record, you still have value in the kingdom of God.

I dedicate this book as a lifeline to those who have found themselves on the opposite end of forever. I do not write this book from my professional expertise as a therapist but rather from the human experiences that God has allowed me to have. However, I believe my ability to remain connected to my human experience improves my professional efficacy.

Therefore, I have extrapolated from my story therapeutic lessons along with corresponding spiritual shifts that created emotional, mental, and spiritual healing for me. At the end of each chapter, you will find these lessons and spiritual shifts as a road map of the healing devised by the Holy Spirit's use from my own painful journey.

In sharing the many lessons learned throughout my journey, I encourage you to take the necessary action to make the spiritual shifts recommended to heal, recover, and grow as women God created, despite the temporary setbacks that life offers each of us. You will also find at the end of the book exhibits A and B describing practical step-by-step instructions to implement God's healing plan and a tool to assist you in avoiding damaging relationships in the future. Exhibit C provides a recommendation for a Christian resource to support you as you traverse the pain and suffering of separation and/ or divorce.

My sister, your story may not completely align with mine, but I have confidence you will find a kindred spirit with all the lessons and spiritual shifts shared within this book.

I am told that the best books are written simultaneously with the wrestle of the author to overcome the very same suffering and trials. If this is true, then you are in for a treat as I draw you into a compelling embrace as we take our journey together. So let's get going.

PART II

The Beginning of Forever

Be willing to let go and exchange your hopes and dreams for God's.

> Why are you downcast, O my soul? Why
> so disturbed within me? Put your hope in God,
> for I will yet praise him, my Savior and my God.
> (Psalm 42:5)

❧ ⸙ ❧

CHAPTER 1

God's Ideal vs. Satan's Raw Deal

What if I told you there could be hope when all fails? By faith, we believe in the ideal marriage that begins with hope and is sustained by true love. We hoped for a marriage that involves the purchase of your first home and plans to fill it with beautiful children. You hope to have many family dinners and entertain family and friends during holidays and special occasions.

Perhaps your hope for daily family devotions and weekly church worship services would be standard operating practices (SOP) in the home. My friend, I wish I could say that all we need is faith, but then I would need to deny or, should I say, defy the reality we live in.

I realize this position I take leaves me stranded out on a shaky limb when I speculate that we were unprepared for the reality that Christian families and marriages can meet the same fate as the secular population. But for the Christian, failed marriages are not the end of our story. It was not the end for Leah (Genesis 29:31–35), and it is not the end for you or me. Please, my sister, believe that you are still valuable to the kingdom of God, even after divorce.

God's Ideal

Therefore a man shall leave his father and
mother and be joined to his wife and they
shall become one flesh (Gen. 2:24)

The beginning of forever opens in the Garden of Eden where God Himself designed and instituted marriage. The Lord formed man of the dust of the ground and breathed the breath of life into his nostrils, and man became a living soul (Genesis 2:7). And believe it or not, this was the first time during the extraordinary six-day process of creation that God declared something was "not good."

He actually said that it was "not good" for man to be alone (Genesis 2:18). So in His good judgment, God decided to "make a helpmeet for him." Amazingly, He began by placing the man in a "deep sleep" (Genesis 2:21) and taking "one of his ribs" and creating a woman and bringing her to the man (Genesis 2:22). Right here is where I stopped in the story and noticed something I had never noticed before.

Don't you just love those "Wake Up Moments" when reading the Bible? This is what I experienced this particular morning. Returning to the garden:

- God identified the loneliness in man and created a helpmeet for him.
- Man was alone, but the woman never experienced loneliness.
- She was created and immediately placed in a relationship with the man.

No wonder, my sister, it feels intolerable when our relationships are broken. We were created for a special purpose with a special nature that reaches its highest satisfaction in harmonious relationship with our mates.

Back to the garden, God created woman out of the flesh and bone of man to indicate the closeness of the union and the strong emotional attachment He intended to exist between them. Listen to the way God puts it:

> For no man ever yet hated his own flesh;
> but nourished and cherished it. (Ephesians 5:29)

> God also commanded that man leave his
> family of origin and cleave to his wife and the
> two shall become one flesh. (Genesis 2:24)

The first Christian marriage stands as a monument to demonstrate the spiritual qualities of companionship and intimacy designed by God Himself to be parallel only to Christ and the Church.

But as you might imagine, sin entered and rewrote the story, but not for long.

Satan's Raw Deal

> If you bite and devour each other,
> watch out or you will be destroyed by
> each other. Galatians 5:15 (NIV)

It was only a few short chapters after the first couple decided to exchange God's Ideal for Satan's Raw Deal. Galatians 5:15 provides the perfect picture of this exchange. Immediately after their encounter with Satan, shame, guilt, and blame entered their world and crowded out the companionship and intimacy of God's ideal for them.

Every kingdom divided against itself will come to ruin. We have the same enemy and have been subjected to the same ruin as Adam and Eve. The two that became one flesh are now two flesh-torn individuals. This tearing away of the flesh is the tortuous nature of divorce. It is very similar to the torture experienced by the separation of death.

At least in death, the person is gone, and the hope of reconciliation ends. In divorce, the hope lingers and persists in suffocating your heart and soul without the promise of relief, a suffocation so debilitating that it causes emotional paralysis.

CHAPTER 2

Emotional Paralysis

Are you familiar with the experience of emotional paralysis? It is the result of losing the breath of hope and becoming immobilized by the Double "D"—Disappointment and Discouragement. Unfortunately, I was introduced to the Double "D" when I realized my marriage was filled with anticipatory joy that was combined with ambiguous security.

Double "D"—Disappointment and Discouragement

My heart desired to eventually marry the man who would love God more than me. I thought his love for God would be the blueprint for loving me, and together, our marriage would glorify God in lifelong service. I believe I must have missed the part where we are to test the spirit to see if it is of God. Everyone calling on the name of Jesus is not His servant.

While there are wives who dream of big homes, cars, and outward displays of wealth, my dream was to be in ministry with my husband. The true "spiritual power couple." I held this dream so tightly that even when faced with contrary evidence, I held on for dear life until it nearly cost me my life (at least my spiritual life). I will say more about this dream as we stay connected on this journey.

There sat the spiritual power couple in church with matching colors. His tie would match the color of my dress, sitting side by side and holding hands during prayer. Aside from this, nothing captivated me more. I wanted the threefold cord union promised in Ecclesiastes 4:12. However, I was not aware of the obvious missing cord.

Now, you would think after experiencing this once or twice, I would have learned my lesson but no, forever the optimist. One year, my Christmas gift from my brother was a clock with a ceramic figurine of a whistling old bum lying on a bench. This theme surfaced quite often in the pattern of my teenage and young adult dating.

My brother was fond of criticizing my choice in men. "Phyllis, you have high hopes," was his mantra. Then later, during a mentor relationship with a high-esteem psychologist, I was advised to allow my dreams to die as an offering to God. But my unrelenting optimism would not allow me to do this.

I continued headstrong forward, sharing my faith with my husband, teaching him to pray, welcoming him into fellowship, and encouraging him in the Lord. But just like a child one week after Christmas, all my efforts flopped once the novelty wore off and he became indifferent and satisfied with a form of godliness instead.

And so my imaginary beginning of forever began to fade into reality. Little did I know that I, too, had exchanged God's Ideal for Satan's Raw Deal by seeking my own way and being unwilling to wait upon the Lord to bring me the mate He had for me.

But know, my sister, that there is good news. When we go our own way and get broken by challenging relationships and circumstances, if we remain soft and pliable in the Father's (or, better yet, in the Potter's) hand, He can mold and shape us into even better vessels than before.

Jesus knows what it is like to be broken by this fallen world and asks us to be of good courage because He has overcome the world and through Him, we too will overcome. *But we have this treasure in earthen vessels, that the excellence of the power may be of God and not of us* (2 Corinthians 4:7).

Investigating challenging relationships and circumstances brings us to Genesis 29:31–35 and introduces us to Leah, whom the Bible referred to as being unloved by her husband (Jacob) regardless of her constant efforts at trying to secure his love. But just like us, Leah had forgotten the great love of God.

With every son she bore, she was sure to have her husband's love and devotion. Her first son, Reuben, represented to her that the Lord looked upon her affliction and knew she was unloved by her husband but still no change in her marriage. She bore again, and this time, she was convinced Jacob would love her, and so she called his name Simeon, but still no change in her marriage.

The third time, she thought, *Surely, three sons would win my husband's love*, and named him Levi but still no change in her marriage. It was not until Leah gave birth to her fourth son, Judah (whose name means "praise"), that she recognized all praises belong to God and pleasing Him should be primary in her life. It was then that she "stopped bearing" the burden of trying to please her husband and secure his love and decided to focus on praising the Lord instead. Can you relate to Leah's desire to effect change in her marriage? I can.

Interestingly, we hear little else about Leah from this point. I believe she found the same spiritual priority of an undivided heart toward God that Ellen G. White (EGW) speaks about in an article entitled, "Separation Better Than Apostasy."

In this article, she recognizes the strong covenantal nature of marital vows. However, she makes the important point that marital vows should never usurp one's spiritual priority and cause "undivided affection" for God (*Testimonies on Sexual Behavior, Adultery, and Divorce*).[3]

Undivided affection is the potency of Satan's tools of condemnation, shame, blame, guilt, disappointment, and discouragement that are so prevalent in the divorce experience. Let me be the first to admit that no one wins in a divorce. Both spouses have failed to honor the marriage vows in one way or another. Awareness of this sinful state is designed to bring repentance that leads to the mercy of God.

Right here is where I struggled. It was not until I acknowledged my part of the failure of the marriage that God's grace began to deliver me. The road signs ahead read, "Accept forgiveness from God." Another sign reads, "Forgive your spouse." Another sign read, "Forgive yourself." These signs pointed toward the tons of hard work, emotional and spiritual healing, and growth to work through.

But I was ready to take the time out to prepare myself for it. I encourage everyone to accept the gift of healing offered by God through His Word, prayer, and satisfying intimacy with Him. Regardless of the degree and assignment of shame, blame, guilt, disappointment, and discouragement proposed by Satan's Raw Deal, an intense, intimate relationship with God is His ideal for you and me.

Lesson learned
Power of compassion

I have learned to ask God for the love and compassion to see my husband in a different way. Acknowledging his woundedness that blinds him to his own sinful behavior, this view of him empowers me to forgive even though reconciliation may be impossible. This view enables me to leave him in God's hands and not mine.

Spiritual shift
Forgive and live

True forgiveness does not always mean reconciliation but is required for the spiritual restoration of my soul. Initially, forgiveness is a choice, then a long-term process that prevents the enemy from filling my heart with hatred and bitterness.

I truly released myself when I entered the arena of forgiveness. Forgiveness is the good fight of faith that promises good soldiers the crown of life (2 Timothy 2:3 and James 1:12). Join me, my friends, this is a worthy fight.

PART III

The Threat of Forever

The gift of goodbye

In everything God works for the good of those who love him (Romans 8:28).

CHAPTER 3

Losing a Dream but Waking Up to Reality

To allow my dream to fade felt like losing command of it. Little did I realize that offering up my dream meant making room to receive God's plan for my life. While I am grateful for the challenges I have survived in my life, this one was most heart-wrenching.

Traveling toward Reality Road

We are about to go down Hope Avenue toward Separation Boulevard and Divorce Drive but not before a right turn into Reality Road. Are we there yet? No.

Be sure to wear your seat belt. We are bound to run into many detours, roadblocks, and obstacles: religious myths, personal opinions, and unkind principles, all of which do not follow biblical travel advisory.

I am reminded of my childhood days of trips from New Jersey to North Carolina with my siblings. After at least five bathroom stops and seven fights over toys and snacks before even reaching Washington, DC, the restless bunch of us would begin repeatedly asking the infamous question that every parent loathes: "Are we there yet?"

Well, I am no longer a child restlessly heading for a physical destination, but I am on a journey toward a spiritual one.

No one can really understand the devastating loneliness of divorce but another suffering companion, not to mention the broken familial and Christian relationships that leave you empty of love and support that were once a certainty. The spiritual disorientation of divorce for a Christian is staggering.

So you can imagine how comforting it was when I discovered Psalms 34:17: *The Lord hears the righteous cry, and He promises to deliver them out of all their troubles.* I am further comforted that, *All things work together for the good of those who love God and are called according to His purpose* (Romans 8:28).

I found my way through this traffic jam wilderness by crying out to the Lord, and He certainly delivered me out of all my trouble. So it becomes my pleasure to take your hand, my sister, as we both cry out to the Lord and find the same deliverance the psalmist found in Psalm 34.

I hear your wobbly words of ambivalence. I have spoken the very same words myself. How do you believe God in the middle of such a devastating experience like divorce or separation? I can promise you that this book will not leave you with pretty little platitudes or Band-Aid scriptures. But my promise to you is that you will find real hope and honesty as I share my divine lessons and spiritual shifts through pain into God's purpose for it all.

He still has great plans for you in His kingdom. How do I know this? Because I am a suffering companion, traveling the same road, and so has our friend, the Samaritan woman of John 4. She was willing to lose a dream and gain reality.

She is gathering water from the well in the middle of the day. She is covered with veils and scarves to conceal her from not only the scorching midday sun but also her shame. See, she has taken several trips down Divorce Drive (five times actually) and met up with some of the same obstacles of religious myths, personal opinions, and unkind principles we face today.

But if we were to follow her entire story, we would find that Jesus took a delightful detour on His journey toward revealing her destiny to finding valuable service to His kingdom. He did not condemn her for the many times her "forever ended" but filled her with the living water of hope. So much so that she left her water jar, exchanging physical water for spiritual renewal.

She decided her testimony did not end with her troubles. She ran into town, no longer veiled with shame but bursting with words of hope, talking about a man who was able to reach in and heal her searching soul. Scripture says that many became believers at her words (John 4:41). She found she still had value to the kingdom of God, and so can we. Since God is not a respecter of persons, there is hope for us.

The hope that our Samaritan friend experienced was not always her story nor has it been mine.

Love and Goodbye

There I stood. Dressed in, if you can believe it, off-white of all colors, long and flowing, veil and everything. What was I thinking? If I were in a court of law, my case would have resolved quickly and I would have been convicted of stupidity with aggravated shame, notwithstanding time served of five years without parole.

Have you ever thought you were making a good decision only to find it was the most disappointing outcome you could have ever imagined? I did. My marriage was such an experience. As I stood there in my off-white wedding gown, my thought was, *Surely, I got it right this time.*

He stood there with the same innocent smile that misled me from day one. I tend to believe a person and offer trust long before it is safe. Where was my woman's intuition? It failed me, or did it?

After returning home from a honeymoon excursion, reality quickly began to rear its dreadful head. Remember, I told you I would return to my dream. Well, there I was still holding onto my dream of having a marriage that would bring glory to God as we minister together in love and service.

Well, things started well. He was a good companion and never afraid to join me in church and Bible study. His smooth conversations with the right words fooled me and all my friends and family members. Because the disguise took everyone in, I was cheered on and given the seal of approval. Little did any of us know or understand the principles of Proverbs 26:23–26:

> Like a coating of silver dross on earthenware
> are fervent lips with an evil heart.
>
> Enemies disguise themselves with their lips
> but in the hearts, they harbor deceit.
>
> Though their speech is charming, do not
> believe them, for seven abominations fill their
> hearts and their malice is concealed by deception.

But praise God for His mercy. The remainder of these verses was also true: "their wickedness will be exposed in the assembly." And this is exactly what started happening. Soon, things stopped adding up. Hidden behind the smile was an entire life lived in secrecy and deception. Marital dedication proved to be as elusive as vapors in the wind. It all seemed surreal until taxed, tested, and tried by the fires of responsibility and commitment.

The Gift of Goodbye

The prospect of having to say goodbye felt like ripping a Band-Aid from an unhealed wound. As a therapist, I know that wounded people require distance from their wrongdoers to process the pain and hurt in order to heal. As a Christian wife, I was forced to accept that there are situations where we must allow our loved one's permission to travel down a road with the Lord that may not include us.

Yes, ladies, Harsh and toxic circumstances may lead to separating from our man but never our God. Yes, sometimes, the gift of goodbye is compulsory. Like Leah, after many unproductive attempts to salvage the relationship, I waved a white flag in surrender to my human, earthly methods. This was a case for the Lord.

While I understood Romans 8:29 and agreed that I am more than a conqueror through Jesus Christ, I felt more like a washed-up basket lady.

When you think of a basket lady, you may picture a very nice lady with a basket full of fruit, cookies, knitting supplies, or some other types of treats but not my basket. My basket was full of the fruit of insecurities and proof of missing the mark. My basket was not filled with goodies but rather with things I wish I could forget. I tried to cover up my basket, even tried to hide it. But it still presented itself fully within my consciousness.

Another biblical friend is also very familiar with a basket of weaknesses and insecurities. He, like us, prayed, prayed, and prayed again for his basket of weaknesses to be transformed into strength and beauty. But our biblical friend found a secret underneath his basket. The Lord showed Paul of Tarsus a secret to his weakness, and that was God's strength.

The Lord is so compassionate and understanding of our true nature. He is fully aware of our baskets of insecurities. So He graciously explains that His strength is made perfect in our weakness. Miraculously, He offers us grace. A grace that is sufficient to overshadow the baskets we carry.

Grace is this wonderful gift basket that runs over but never out. This basket is filled with the goodies of life that will fortify our human weaknesses and glorify God at the same time. I chose to focus on the power of God rather than my human weaknesses (2 Corinthians 12:10).

I share my story with you because I know what it is like to love someone and have to leave them. I know the pain of relinquishing a dream that has been yours for as long as you can remember. I know what it's like to lose someone and never find the closure you need. I can identify with the loneliness that crowds your life with its presence and threatens your "forever."

Sharon Adler coined the questions flooding my mind at this point in my marriage:

> Why didn't God warn me? Why did he let me waste my time and emotions on someone so insufferably untrustworthy, someone who would change his feelings toward me so easily? Wasn't my marriage ordained? Am I supposed to stick it out because of my vows, for better or worse? Why can't God fix this person's illness if He values families staying together?[4]

I know the same questions flood your mind as well. You are not alone. I have been here several times. I am not proud to report this, but I desperately sought peace in the human heart of a man. I know now where true Peace resides. In fact, I learned that peace is not a feeling nor a state of mind. Peace is the person of Jesus Christ (Isaiah 9:6).

Lesson learned
Learning who is leading in times of trouble

God often leads His people through the wilderness to get to the promised land (Exodus 14–16). God does not cause the wilderness experience. He is leading us through the wilderness of brokenness, barrenness, and emptiness of destructive marriages. I learned to look for the lessons in the wilderness. They will be important to take into the promised land.

Spiritual shift
Handling wilderness moments

Learning to take comfort in the middle ground between the wilderness and the promised land. Sometimes, the blessings are found in the pain that we must walk through. This is where we will find Jesus intently at work preparing our souls for heaven. Bread will fall from heaven to feed us during times of famine in our lives here on earth.

Exodus 16:35 is proof of God's provision and deliverance during our wilderness moments. Let us burst out into song with Moses: *The Lord is my strength and song, and He has become my salvation; He is my God and I will praise Him; The Lord is a man of war; the Lord is His name* (Exodus 15:2, 3).

CHAPTER 4

Searching for Love in Human Hearts

This is my personal story. The year I lost my father, I lost my marriage. It makes sense because they were intricately entwined. I never really found my father. So in essence, I never really found the marriage I thought I had. Blinded by pain and ignorant of suffering, I was confused on both accounts.

It starts with a little girl looking to feel loved and secured. She moved from house to house and spent long days walking and searching for one small glimpse of her father. She would be lucky on occasion and find him at his auto garage, headfirst under the hood of a car or truck.

He would be greasy and smelly, but oh, how she would relish in the aroma of her dad. His overalls were covered in grease. His hands were black from soot. She would stand by, hoping to get a peek of his greasy face or, better yet, have him notice the longing in her heart for his attention. There she would stand, watching the back of his head, engrossed in some repair.

On occasion, he would lift himself, wipe his hands, and pull her into a sweaty, smelly embrace. If it was a good visit, he would show affection by picking at the pimples on her teenage acne-filled face.

Oh, how this meager display of affection would satisfy the deepest need she carried.

Before she could complete adolescence, her father would have chosen another family, had another daughter, and rarely showed his face again. It was not until her late twenties that he would occasionally return on holidays. She was rarely called on birthdays even though she was born the on same week of his own birthday.

There were many broken promises of visits, attendance at graduations and weddings, etc. But despite it all, she was known to be a "daddy's girl." She forbade anyone from speaking against her father, regardless of its truth. She was the starch defender of the one who abandoned and rejected her most of her life.

Eventually, she began to confuse the love with the pain in her heart. On some level, she experienced them both the same. This makes sense because the one she loved the most hurt her the most. She carried this identity with her into adulthood as she stumbled into various replications of her father in the arms of toxic relationships.

They all have different names but the same personality—fake. They were all men with their backs to her, engrossed in their selfishness, willing to offer only a meager display of affection that she was so accustomed to receiving from her father. And when they would hurt her, she would only confuse it with love and work hard to defend them to avoid the abandonment and rejection that were sure to follow or perhaps already there.

It was not until the year of her father's death that she was finally able to lay to rest the painful journey of a lifetime. As God would have it, before his death, he became ill and had to live with her for many months, while she nursed him back to health. This gift was illustrative of the love and care he denied her. And somehow, this brought healing to her heart.

But her father's death brought about another death. The death of another dream of experiencing true love from a man. The eye-opening experience is amazing. Once your eyes are open, you cannot close them in ignorance again. Once she could *see* her father, she *saw* her current husband. He, too, has another life. He is also bent over the hood, hiding and engrossed in a life separate from her.

Again, she sees herself standing by waiting for any show of real commitment to a love relationship that extends beyond the surface and shadows of broken promises, another selfish man who looks only after his own needs.

Likewise, the journey of pain, abandonment, and rejection began again as it was with her father. It has a new color, flavor, and scent but the same old confusion of pain for love again. She continues the journey…spending lots of time, searching for one small glimpse of her husband who is not there.

Lysa TerKeurst said it best when sharing her personal story of the challenging relationship with her father:

> When a man is physically present but emotionally absent, a girl's heart can feel quite hollow and helpless. This is true whether that man is her father, her husband, or even a man whom she deeply respects.[5]

There is good news. Praise the Lord for good news! I have another faithful and trustworthy Father who loves me with everlasting love. I have another Husband who promises to care for me as He does the sparrows in the sky. Sometimes, I forget to hold people in this life loosely. I sometimes forget that people are flawed (just as I am), and disappointment and discouragement are intermittent companions in this life.

Lesson learned

Move away from men (or people in general) that will take pleasure in receiving more than they are willing to provide.

Spiritual shift

It is important to explore childhood events that may be blinding us from current issues in life. For me, it was a well-established habit of ignoring the bad behavior of men in my life. Jesus does not ignore bad behavior. It cost Him His life.

The cross is a symbol that sin cannot be excused, overlooked, or ignored in my life, your life, or that of others. I now understand this principle and am able to allow my father to rest in peace and appropriately grieve the loss of my marriage so that I can also rest in peace (more about grief in Chapter 6).

PART IV

The Shame of Forever

Broken vows

We learn from failure, not from success.
(Dracula, Bram Stoker)

CHAPTER 5

Broken Vows

God's perfect timing forced the growth of my faith. Can you imagine facing a broken marriage on Valentine's Day of all days? It was difficult to escape the stark contrast of a broken marriage amid a day that radiates with love. Love was displayed in every television commercial, most sitcoms, and news reports and across all social media platforms, just what I needed, continuous stabbing in the unprotected, gaping wound in my heart.

The most significant infirmity of divorce is the attached stigma of "shame." The last thing a Christian woman wants to be labeled as is *a failure.* Divorce, regardless of fault, feels so much like failure. I recall the day it hit me hard. Day after day, I lay around, sulking and telling my mother that I was such a failure.

The day arrived when she had had enough. I have one of those mothers who raised strong Christian daughters alone as a single mother. She did not allow us the luxury of self-pity. So upon hearing my declaration of failure, she firmly said to me, "Your marriage failed, yes, but you are not a failure."

Now, you must try to imagine her no-nonsense tone, stern facial expression, and both-hands-on-hip stance. She had not spent most of her life raising me to be intelligent, independent, and resourceful to allow me to willingly give in to weakness.

It worked and shook me out of my "poor me" attitude. But it took several months for me to learn how to be disappointed and how to let failure produce resilience, generate growth, and initiate change in my life.

Dr. Brené Brown has researched extensively about shame over many years. She defines shame as "the intensely painful feeling or experience of believing we are flawed and therefore unworthy of acceptance and belonging." She also rightly believes that telling our stories breaks the power of shame.6 She could have very well been describing the divorce experience The fear of disconnection that underlies shame makes divorce intolerable.

Necessary Separation

I found it difficult to shake the shame of my diligent efforts to maintain my marriage to no avail. I wished him to change. I willed him to change. I prayed for his change. I exhausted myself with his change that never seemed to preface the horizon. "Every glimmer of change" came with such flickering hope. My heart was broken. My fairy tale did not include the knight in shining armor, but instead, I ended up having to armor myself with a necessary separation.

Through years of personal counseling and professional training as a therapist, I knew that I entered the marriage with a healthy sense of self and purpose. However, the mortification of another broken marriage was too much to bear. There were many instances where I had to sort through the lies, secrecy, and deception that were becoming a mainstay in my current marriage.

Because of this, the enemy had a foothold to zap my strength and leave me on unstable ground. I needed to pull away long enough to allow the Holy Spirit access to my heart and mind for healing and restoration, a necessary separation. The purpose of separation is not only for healing of the wounded but also in hopes of waking the unrepentant spouse to the destructiveness of his/her ways. This became my daily prayer.

Shame of Unfaithfulness

I am no formal researcher, but if I were to take a stab at a definition of *shame*, it would read something like this: *a feeling of inadequacy and failure to become all that you want to be and all that God has created you to be.* The painful work of overcoming shame takes the courage to rewrite your story.

The enemy has offered a script of failure, unworthiness, and unlovability. And he wants us to live with it in secrecy and to hide in shame. He hates it when we dare retell the story laced with the grace of God, the Author and Finisher of our faith story (Hebrews 12:2).

To retell my grace-filled story, I continued to wrestle with God. The question God and I wrestled with was, "How and why did my efforts to save my marriage met with unfaithful scorn?" Perhaps you are familiar with this wrestling with God. All I wanted was what God promised—a "one-flesh" relationship. Why was it so difficult?

Israel's Unfaithfulness

Judges Chapters 11–16

I imagined the Lord understood my frustration with the cyclical pattern of sin in my marriage. The Lord dealt with Israel's rebellion for 350 years—seven cycles of apostasy with His people beginning with Judges 3 through 16. Reading these chapters shows a sense of true and false repentance.

True repentance is more than a feeling of sorrow for sin but an actual change resulting in the action of turning away from it. Several times in this passage, the Lord's soul was grieved with the generation of people who did not know Him, but He continued to offer salvation and restoration. Everyone must make a personal decision to have a relationship with God, to love Him and keep His commandments.

This is personal work. Salvation is individual work. I was trying to do something for my husband that only he can do by exercising his own free will. I noticed that for each period in the book of Judges, the people had to make true repentance before any restoration of their relationship to the Lord. Repentance is the antidote to relational restoration.

Marital Accountability

Marital accountability is the corrective, redemptive approach to win the erring soul in toxic marriages. The church's responsibility to respond to those broken by separation/divorce should be equal to the response to those broken by the death of a spouse.

This sort of spiritual support for those suffering toxicity in marriage can be life-changing to many people. But when all fail and your spouse exercises free will to reject the healing opportunity of church discipline and marital accountability, unfortunately, separation and/ or divorce may very well be the unwanted yet realistic outcome.

If this is your reality as it was mine, please know that God can and will never leave you nor divorce His righteous ones. His love is truly everlasting and endures forever. He doesn't hate divorced people. He hates the damaging effects of divorce upon the family, community, and especially His church. It is truly the plan of the enemy to deface marriage because it represents Christ and His church, the bride.

This is the painful side of life here under the sun. Believe me when I tell you no one rejoices in these circumstances. Delicacy and sensitivity are necessary for all concerned. Judgment and advice-giving and well-meaning people would do well to turn their hearts toward heaven and bring these hurting brothers and sisters to the throne of grace where mercy can be dispensed in healing abundance. We will address more about how the church can be a blessing to these families later.

Lesson learned

For sharing this lesson learned, I will use the words of Leslie Vernick: "Healing a destructive marriage can never be the sole responsibility of one person in the relationship. It always takes two people willing to work to achieve godly change."[7]

Leslie Vernick is a Christian counselor and author who is gifted with spiritual discernment to share biblical truth about toxicity in marriage from a sensitive, practical yet responsible perspective.

Spiritual shift

In a marriage, both have a spiritual responsibility to God and one another. However, that responsibility is not a license to subjugate personal accountability to accept sinful behavior. I am learning to refuse to relinquish my spiritual responsibility to hold my spouse accountable for sinful behavior. It serves no one to allow sin to go unnoticed.

My friends, take note of how Jesus dealt with Zaccheus and the way He lovingly confronted Cain (more about this later).

✦

PART V

The End of Forever

Earthly failures reveal the faithfulness of God.

> "For the LORD God of Israel says
>
> That He hates divorce,
>
> For it covers one's garment with violence,"
>
> Says the LORD of hosts. (Malachi 2:16)

CHAPTER 6

"Great Is Your Faithfulness"

Throughout this book, you have heard me reference my refusal to release my dream. Well, let me confess. I was not able to live until my dream was dead. I wrote a eulogy and held a funeral for my dream. Yes, it may sound strange, but I had to convince my heart and head that the dream was dead.

Kübler-Ross's stages of grief were life-giving to me. I lived in *denial* for decades, smoothing over my *anger*, and sought to *bargain* with life too often to recall. It was not until I allowed *depression* to fully express itself that *acceptance* began to rise and set me free.[8]

Healing slowly began to surface as I allowed myself to grieve and recover from the loss. Galatians 2:20 became my life verse and a fitting dedication to my dream's funeral: *I have been crucified with Christ; it is no longer I who live, but Christ lives in me; and the life which I now live in the flesh I live by faith in the Son of God, who loved me and gave Himself for me.*

Both my dream and I were crucified with Christ, and now, I live by faith in the God who loves me and sacrificed Himself for me. This is the kind of love relationship that ended my earthly search of forever in the arms of human flesh.

The End of Forever was the Beginning of Never. Never again would I offer myself on the altar of broken vows. Never again would I accept a dream that was not handpicked by God, Himself. Like Leah in Genesis 29:35, I finally gave birth to my praise (Judah) and stopped bearing the burden of brokenness. Like the Samaritan woman from John 4, I dropped my pot of worldly water offered by men and began drinking from the well of water that will never run dry.

There is no more shame and unyielding high hopes for earthly relationships, but rather, I now hold on to the blessed hope found in Jesus Christ. Why seek advice from the world of well-meaning people when the Word of God is filled with guidance and direction, healing, and regeneration.

In Christ, I am loved with an everlasting love, and underneath are His everlasting arms. "The eternal God is your refuge, and underneath is the everlasting arms" (Deuteronomy 33:27). Now, is this not what we are looking for, ladies? Everlasting love with everlasting arms? A refuge from the hurt and pain of toxic relationships?

Practically speaking, there are times when an ending is the beginning of the comfort and compassion we deserve. This type of surrender leaves an opportunity for the Lord to give us His choice for a mate. We see this played out in the life and story of Abigail from 1 Samuel 25.

She was married to a surely (foolish) man. She, too, was a product of a toxic marriage. However, she remained full of grace and dignity regardless of what was going on in her life. There can be no growth or fruitfulness in a life that is centered in self.[9]

The secret of Abigail's character was not found in the self-pity I was rolling around in. Rather, it was found in her connection to her Lord. She maintained daily communication in the sweet language of God's Word. This is where I eventually discovered it as well. I called this process "finding your life verses."

A life verse is just what it sounds like. Scripture verses breathe into my soul the necessary life and movement that reverse the emotional paralysis that was slowly becoming my norm. My mind was locked in prison chains, much like those that held Paul and Silas. Their chains were broken by the power of prayer and praise in Acts 16:25–34, so were mine, and so can yours.

I invite you to make some of my life verses your own. I learned to personalize the Word of God to make it easier to digest pain and nourish my soul.

Life verse #1

I will never forget the day I discovered Isaiah 55:5–10. I was sitting on my living room floor, blinded by my familiar friends: tears and sadness. You know, those friends who overstay their welcome, and all you can do is hope and pray they would receive a phone call that would summon them somewhere else, anywhere but with you.

I was not so blessed. So I resigned myself to endure another evening with my unwanted guests. But this time, I decided to read my Bible seeking some much-needed comfort. I read in Isaiah 55:10 that God's Word is as faithful and sure as the rain and snow waters the earth before returning to heaven. I thought about this analogy and could not come up with any evidence of when it would rain or snow and not water the earth. This is the day that confidence in God's Word took a stronghold in my soul, and I never forgot that moment. I hope you never forget it either.

Life verse #2

Isaiah 41:10 is another one of those verses that can uphold you when earth's failures meet with the faithfulness of my God. The words "fear not" can be found 365 times in Scripture—one for every day of the year. So then, daily, I am reminded that God is with me to strengthen, help, and uphold me with His righteous right hand.

How could I fear, reminding myself of this promise daily? What about you?

Life verse #3

Now if you have ever been the brunt of evildoers, Psalm 37 will sing you to sleep at night. It is impossible to read Psalm 37, all forty verses, without facing a faithful God who is totally trustworthy and promises justice and righteousness when others successfully carry out their wicked schemes.

What if divorced women held onto this promise and continued to trust in the Lord and do good? What if they chose to delight themselves in the Lord and rest patiently as they commit to Him? What if they would believe that He would not only order their steps but also deliver them from the wicked one?

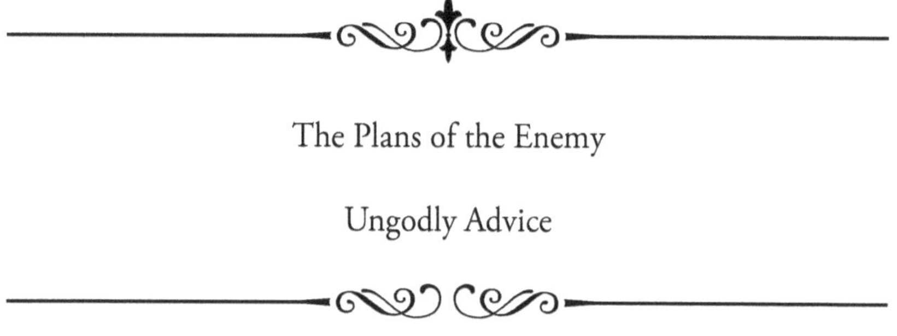

The Plans of the Enemy

Ungodly Advice

Earthly Failures

Early on, I shared with you my brokenhearted concern for the lack of spiritual support and comfort from the church to minister the love of Christ to broken families of divorce and separation. This is not from a position of harsh judgment but heartfelt pain from personal experience. I recognize it to be the plan of the enemy and not purposeful pain from others.

Unfortunately, some of the most ungodly advice comes from the lips of the people of God. I am convinced that people mean well and have good intentions. I received such unreasonable advice when a good friend of mine laid such a heavy burden upon me that culminated in several more years of enduring emotional abuse in my marriage.

She meant well, and I still love her for her interest in me and my Christian witness. But what I needed most was an empathetic heart, a listening ear, and loads and loads of prayer. Another close church sister took it upon herself to launch a campaign in favor of my spouse without ever consulting, comforting, or campaigning for me. Many others played into the plans of the enemy to pour oil on the already blazing fire of pain and suffering.

Another painful experience occurred when I was brought before a tribunal of the pastor and elders to discuss the continuation of my leadership position. At the same time, my spouse was selected to preach on two separate occasions. I was forced to listen to church members' opinions of the eloquence of his sermons, while no one stopped long enough to listen to me.

Granted, I refused to exploit the privacy of my marital issues, and this loyalty cost me the support of many brothers and sisters in Christ and exposed me to gossip and character assassination. I think I cried for weeks afterward.

But I held onto the promise of the Lord that informed me that the righteous will never be put to shame. *Do not let me be put to shame, nor let my enemies triumph over me. No one whose hope is in you will ever be put to shame, but they will be put to shame who are treacherous without excuse* (Psalm 25:1 NIV).

EGW demonstrates the most practical advice I have ever heard on the subject of necessary separation or apostasy, when she wrote:

One of the gravest mistakes one can make in life is to permit oneself to be controlled by Satan through the device of a spouse who has yielded themselves into the hands of Satan and the marriage has become a snare of Satan to render one unfitted for the kingdom. The marriage vow that binds the husband to the wife must remain unbroken, but he [she] has also vowed to his (her) Lord, to love Him with the whole heart, the undivided affection.[10]

Let me be the first to apologize to you, my sister, for any well-meaning and heartbreaking counsel you may have experienced as well. It takes spiritual discernment and insight into the nature of a troubled marriage to fully understand the damage to the spiritual life of its members. Scripture bears this out:

But if the unbeliever departs, let him depart; a brother or a sister is not under bondage in such cases. But God has called us to peace. For how do you know, O wife, whether you will save your husband? Or how do you know, O husband, whether you will save your wife? (1 Corinthians 7:15, 16)

Unfortunately for some of us, it takes spiritual discernment to be able to define "unbelievers" when they sit in the same pews as the rest of the congregation. I say "unfortunately" because we do not always find this type of "spiritual discernment" in our churches.

Lesson learned

There are no cookie-cutter marriages, so then how can there be cookie-cutter responses to all marriage problems? You cannot take the same paintbrush to color all marriages. The amazing thing I learned in this journey is that the love of Christ and His Word are extremely relevant, revolutionary, and redemptive to all His children and every problem they face. My life verses are proof of this.

Spiritual shift

Live wholeheartedly for Jesus as a protective measure against the snares of Satan.

PART VI

The Hope of Forever

Just when we think all is over, God is just getting started, shifting focus from hurt to hope with the promises of God.

CHAPTER 7

Misuse of Scripture

Suffering Gone Too Far

First Corinthians 7:10 is not intended to cause secondary trauma. Even God calls for healthy boundaries—see Psalm 101:7. How can it be the will of God to allow destructive behavior from another Christian, especially when it is a spouse? To remain silent is to collaborate with evil and sin rather than confront it.

The objective is to offer the responsible party the opportunity to repent and be redeemed. The Lord provided His promises to guide us, not for us to guide His promises. Misuse of Scripture can be traumatizing to those already suffering enormously.

God sets boundaries, and He taught me to do the same thing. I am hoping you will learn by reading this book that boundary setting is a healthy and appropriate response to sin wherever it is discovered and within any relationship.

You may also wonder what is a true consequence and whether they are even appropriate or godly? Jeremiah 7:8–34 and Genesis 4 set forth biblical boundaries and associated consequences. The first is God's approach to erring Judah and Israel.

He was forced to "cast them out of His sight," describing their behavior as "trusting in lying words" and *engaging in* "stealing, murder, adultery, swearing falsely, and living in unfaithfulness," such as "burning incense unto Baal and walking after other gods whom they did not know."

I can hear the grief and the quenching of the Holy Spirit. Can you? God sets boundaries and applies appropriate consequences when necessary. Keep reading.

The latter is where we get to eavesdrop on the spiritual counsel God gave to Cain. So gently, he says to Cain: "Why are you angry? And why has your countenance fallen? If you do well, will you not be accepted? And if you do not do well, sin lies at the door. And its desire is for you, but you should rule over it."

Unfortunately, even with such loving counsel and a chance to redeem himself, Cain ignored God and eventually killed his brother. When the Lord approached again for a final chance to repent, Cain dug his stubborn and unrepentant feet deeper and complained about the consequences of his actions.

Cain says, "My punishment is greater than I can bear!" Believe it or not, instead of feeling guilt over killing his brother, Cain was more concerned for his own life as a fugitive and being recognized as a vagabond on the earth.

Selfishness and self-centeredness occur in all marriages on some level. However, when selfishness is aggressive and eradicates the emotional, mental, or spiritual safety in the marriage, things have gone too far, using Scripture to keep anyone in such an emotionally damaging environment cannot be sanctioned by the God of the Bible. His word provide many instructions on how to treat one another as well as how to deal with sin in the camp (James 5:19, Ephesians 5:11, and Psalm 120:1, 2).

Misinterpretations of Grace

Should grace cover serious and painful behavior? Should love cover a multitude of sins? Yes, love is a mercy requirement, and grace is unmerited favor, no doubt.

In the above conversation between the Lord and Cain, He informed Cain that sin lies at his door and seeks to overrule his soul. But Cain rejected the grace boundary the Lord provided him and therefore had to suffer natural consequences of his decision.

Israel followed Judah into ignoring the grace boundary and suffered oppression and captivity because "the nation would not obey the voice of the Lord their God nor receive correction" (Jeremiah 7:28). Again, God sets boundaries. God applies consequences.

Psalm 107 warns that He will not strive with us forever either. Grace is not misrepresented in Scripture; it is misapplied by the people of Scripture. You would be hard-pressed to find a Christian who would agree that grace is a license to sin. But it requires enough spiritual discernment to appropriately apply grace in difficult situations. Unfortunately, this is where the church falls short.

Spiritual confrontation is outlined in Scripture at Galatians 6:1–2. There is never a good reason to overlook the sin and personal struggles of church members. We are called to do that exact opposite. Confront rather than shy away under the guise of privacy and fail to ask the difficult questions that could lead to restorative instruction.

Galatians 6:1 says, "If sin has become evident, simply deal with it." Jesus never ignored sin. One would only need to read Matthew 23 to see His approach with the Pharisees (self-righteousness). The goal of this spiritual confrontation is to gently "restore" your erring brother or sister. I recently read an article on point written by Pastor Brad Larson where he said the following:

Jesus speaks into every condemning reality with grace, since He has borne all condemnation for those who trust him. Hard conversations can be gospel conversations. So while your guts may churn, your heart can also leap for joy at what God might do.[11]

What if the church bore one another's burdens and so fulfilled the law of Christ as Scripture encourages it to do? I believe showing up for both parties in a destructive marriage would be modeling the same ministry of love and truth that Jesus displayed when He was here. He is love, but He also describes Himself as truth. It serves no one when we chose to separate the two.

Lesson learned

It is easy to misuse Scripture by reading into it what we already believe. Rather, we want to allow Scripture to be our belief system (2 Timothy 2:15).

Spiritual shift

To appropriately apply grace with spiritual discernment requires I talk to Jesus before opening my mouth to others. I am instructed to remember that here on earth, I only see dimly, and my own understanding can be darkened by my own pride and prejudices (Proverbs 3:5–6).

—❧ ❧—

CHAPTER 8

The Church's Response

The church is right when it upholds marriage vows and covenants. The church is right when it advocates that the real enemy is not our spouses. The church makes a good point when it upholds grace and forgiveness.

The church falls short at razor blade scriptures without true spiritual discernment of the nature and damage of toxic marriages. The church falls short of offering advice without comfort and compassion.

Malachi 2:16 counsels the church on the Lord's disdain for divorce. He tells us why He hates divorce because "it (divorce) covers one's garment with violence." There is a certain spiritual discernment necessary to distinguish between the issue of divorce and the people involved in the divorce.

The guidance of Ellen G. White comes to light again when she wrote of the consequence of hasty marriages: "even among the professed people of God, there are separations, divorces, and great confusion in the church."[12]

This "great confusion" causes unintended vicarious abuse for divorced people in general and women in particular. What do I mean by this? I shared earlier about some unsavory advice I received from a well-meaning friend that caused me to endure additional years of suffering because of the mishandling of the sensitive issues involved in marital difficulties.

Divorce is classified as one of the most profound crises of faith. Facing the end of any marriage, toxic or not, one experiences loss of confidence in their judgment, their spouse, and often in God who chose not to prevent the loss. Peter was very familiar with such a crisis of faith when he denied Jesus three times after declaring his undying commitment a few moments earlier (Luke 22:54–62).

Many of us have similarly declared our undying love and commitment to our intended at the wedding altar, only to find we, like Peter, are shamefully looking into the face of Jesus when the marriage begins to break down. I know how Peter must have felt. Nothing is more agonizing than to know that you have dishonored God with your life witness.

Therefore, I consider it treacherous to have the church's disapproval to contend with as well. But again, Jesus paints another picture. He met with Peter after His resurrection. He sought him out to offer mercy in response to his failure (Mark 14:33–42). Oh, how I wish His church would follow suit.

Leaving a destructive marriage cannot be an unpardonable sin. Can it? Perhaps separation is an act of faith rather than an act of sin. Let's dig a little deeper in our search without petty partial prejudices.

I wonder what needless pain could have been forfeited by mimicking the following advice by Ellen G. White in another letter to a hurting wife who separated from a toxic marriage:

> *I cannot advise you to return to D unless you
> see decided changes in him.* The Lord is not pleased
> with the ideas he has had in the past of what is

due to a wife… If he holds to his former views, the future would be not better for you than the past has been. He does not know how to treat a wife. I feel very sad about this matter. I feel indeed sorry for D, *but I cannot advise you to go to him against your judgment.* I speak to you as candidly as I spoke to him; it would be perilous for you to again place yourself under his dictation. I had hoped that he would change…

The Lord understands all about your experiences… Be of good courage in the Lord; He will not leave you nor forsake you. *My heart goes out in tenderest sympathy for you.*

I advise that these unfortunate ones be left to God and their own consciences, and that the church shall not treat them as sinners until they have evidence that they are such in the sight of the holy God. He reads hearts as an open book. He will not judge as man judgeth[13] (emphasis mine).

What a balance of grace and truth! Judgment and advice were unnecessary. Comfort and sympathy for suffering were necessary. What if the church left divorce or separated people to God and their own consciences and did not treat them as sinners (without evidence)?

God can read hearts, and He is the only one able to judge righteously. This is particularly important in physically, emotionally, or psychologically destructive marriages.

You can never go wrong by bringing these sufferers to God in prayer and sympathy. The church specializes in reconciliation—reconciling people to God, not to evildoers.

What if both parties in a divorce or separation were treated with equal measures of grace and truth? What if both parties would meet with the same offer of restoration as Peter found with Jesus during his great crisis of faith? What if churches offered broken families a shelter of safety and joined them in their fight against the common enemy? What if we used our words to pray rather than to judge and criticize?

Dear Lord of All Comfort:

We bring before you this family facing the worst of all disappointments. Lord, bless them to find You in their pain. Your loving care for this family can heal their hurt and restore their souls. Help them to release anger, resentment and bitterness, refusing to allow the enemy a foothold. We know the enemy's scheme to bring shame and cause either party to hide in isolation. Help us, Lord, to have love enough to cover a multitude of sins so that all members of this family can experience our love and support. Forgive us, God, when we have judged and criticized, rightfully or wrongfully, leaning to our own understanding. You and You alone know the plans you have for this family and we know those plans are to bring good and not evil to all concerned. Our eyes are upon You Lord to bring Your will center focused for this family and may they release their will in exchange for Yours. In Jesus Name, Amen

Just reading this prayer brings such comfort and peace to my heart. I wrote it as a template for the church to support these families and encourage the church to refrain from transposing their views and opinions without knowledge and understanding.

Lesson learned

There is a way that seems right to a man, but the end thereof leads to destruction (Proverbs 14:12). Opinions are just opinions and should be repudiated by God's Word.

Spiritual shift

Prayer changes everything, and everything is changed by prayer. The prayer approach will relinquish the pride and presumptive pronouncements of blame and shame.

Delightful Detours

When life takes wrong turns, God has U-turns. We must choose to heal by trusting God even when life takes unexpected detours. The unexpected detours could be a broken marriage, lost job, elderly parent's dementia, hostile work environments, etc. I can relate to all the above.

Join me in trusting God when facing the end of forever wondering where to turn next. Our missed opportunities could become our ministry. We can and will find that there remain a purpose and plan for our lives and service to our heavenly Father.

Hope in God

King Solomon was considered the wisest man to ever live. But even then, he had to learn the same trust lessons as we do now. His trust lessons led him to pen the words of Lamentations 3:20–24:

> My soul still remembers and sinks within me. This I recall to my mind, Therefore I have hope. Through the LORD's mercies, we are not consumed, Because His compassions fail not. They are new every morning; Great is Your faithfulness. "The LORD is my portion," says my soul, "Therefore I hope in Him!"

I imagine you are just as excited as I am to know that the Lord shows up every morning with new mercies for the day. There are still mornings that I wake up with a sinking sense of the unknown, and the future appears to be beyond my ability to influence change.

I remind myself that I can take another breath and then another one until I am filled with the courage to hope in God's faithfulness in delightful detours. I call them delightful because they always lead to pleasant pursuits of God that were unintended but essential to the growth and development of my character.

God never wastes a worry, and He always shows up when I think He is not looking. His eyes are always upon the righteous to deliver him from all his troubles. Thank God for that.

There Should Be Some "Buts" in Your Life

You cannot follow Jesus without "buts." If when we are down, we are out, then we will need to give up now. I know you are not ready to throw in the proverbial towel, and neither am I. So can I come closer to you as I encourage us both with 2 Corinthian4:8–9: "We are hard-pressed on every side, yet not crushed; we are perplexed, *but* not in despair; persecuted, *but* not forsaken; struck down, *but* not destroyed" (emphasis mine).

Comfort in Suffering

How can we minister to the divorced or separated? We offer marriage counseling, family counseling, grief counseling, etc. Suffering comes in all assortments and dimensions with specified length and breadth of life stressors. As a body of Christ, 2 Corinthians 1:3–5 should not just be the theme scripture of this book but the watchword of the Christian faith:

Blessed be the God and Father of our Lord
Jesus Christ, the Father of mercies and God of

all comfort, who comforts us in all our tribulation, that we may be able to comfort those who
are in any trouble, with the comfort with which
we ourselves are comforted by God. For as the
sufferings of Christ abound in us, so our consola-
tion also abounds through Christ.

What would be SMART goals and objectives of ministering to
the divorced or separated? Consider the below:

S: Share specific promises of God.
M: Measure by spiritual discernment rather than personal opinion.
A: Attend to all parties concerned without partiality.
R: Remember to pray for God's will over human desires.
T: Trust God with His plans for the family, and know that some-
    times, it may be very different from what is expected by human
    knowledge.

Lesson learned

I am learning to see delightful detours as routes to overcome life's
disappointments. Interestingly though, the idea that a failed marriage
is a delightful detour is equally intriguing as the notion that there is an
end of forever. What detours are you facing today, and what routes do
you need to correct to find the hope and comfort of God?

Spiritual shift

Moving from worry to worship in the face of disappointments
forces us to search deeper for the faithfulness of God. I have no shame
in sharing with you that this particular spiritual shift for me has been
most difficult to make.

There are still days that my fight with fear wins the battle but
not the war. Like David, let us daily open windows wide to offer
prayer, praise, and thanksgiving to a hearing and very-present God.

PART VII

The Eternal Forever

Feeling eternally loved

Let us be glad and rejoice and give Him glory, for the marriage of the Lamb has come, and His wife has made herself ready." And to her it was granted to be arrayed in fine linen, clean and bright, for the fine linen is the righteous acts of the saints. (Revelation 19:7, 8)

CHAPTER 10

Bride of Christ

Remember the wedding made in heaven we have always dreamed of as girls? We dreamed of wearing the perfect white dress that would dazzle the room upon our entrance to the wedding, the oohs and ahhs from the audience, the beam of love in the eyes of our groom waiting at the altar.

We have long awaited for this moment, and everything good and thrilling fill the very fiber of our being. How could this end in disaster? A thought that would dare not enter our mind but has the audacity to invade our world.

Revelations 19:7, 8 redeems this dream for us. I do not know about you, but I want to invest my time in readiness for becoming the bride of Christ prepared to be married to the Lamb of God. I am interested in trading in my perfect white dress for the fine linen, bright and clean arrayed for the eternal marriage where I will be eternally loved. I want to be adorned in garments of a righteousness character resulting from intimate and everlasting fellowship with Jesus Christ.

Forever Restored

Until His return, I will enjoy this intimate and everlasting fellowship with a Husband who loves His imperfect bride and sacrificed

Himself for me. Both you and I will finally enjoy a marriage that will not end in disaster but one that will transcend time and usher in eternity.

We will have a Husband that creates a mansion for us to live in His presence forever—the new heaven, new earth, and New Jerusalem revealed to John coming out of heaven from God:

> Prepared as a bride adorned for her husband… Behold, the tabernacle of God is with men, and He will dwell with them, and they shall be His people. God, Himself will be with them and be their God. And God will wipe away every tear from their eyes; there shall be no more death, nor sorrow, nor crying. There shall be no more pain, for the former things have passed away. (Revelations 21:2–5)

I know for a fact that every tear shed by myself and many of my divorced and separated friends will be wiped away—no more sorrow of brokenness of heart, no more pain of separation and shame. All these experiences will pass away and make room for the new things that our heavenly Bridegroom is preparing for His bride.

Are you preparing for the most important wedding of all? Can you declare with me the final words of the Book? "Even so, come, Lord Jesus!"

E X H I B I T   A

God's Healing Plan

Dear sister, I am grateful to you for taking the time to listen to my story. I hope there was something in it that stirred you toward seeking your own healing. I would have drowned in the sorrow of losing my marriage had Jesus not thrown in a few lifesavers—lifesavers of practical coping strategies to stabilize my pain. The one reassurance He continued to provide was that He cared just as much about my mental and spiritual condition as my marital condition. I wish I could say that all marriages will be saved. But this would be equal to pedaling pipe dreams rather than acknowledging and accepting the reality of living in this world of sin. This was a hard pill for me to swallow, and I know it is choking you as well. Scripture informs us, "What God has joined together, let no man put asunder" (Mark 10:9). The optimal word in that last sentence is *God*. Does God enjoin people in damaging and destructive marriages that cause emotional, mental, and spiritual brokenness at the unrepentant hands of broken people? My prayer is that this message is not misinterpreted to advocate for the frivolity of divorce. Marriage remains honorable to God, as well as to me. I am still a believer in the sanctity of marriage as God designed it, even after having my heart broken time and time again. I am determined not to join the bandwagon of blame, no matter how tempting it can be. However, the reality remains that even with my best of intentions and that of all my godly married sisters everywhere, divorce is sometimes an unwanted ending of our forever. And other times, we are called upon to find joy amid unhappy marriages through praying for the perseverance that may lead to spiritual growth and maturity for both parties. I would caution you to be prayerful about which journey the Lord is calling you. But we are not referencing mere "unhappy marriages" in this book. Sound spiritual discernment is necessary to make the distinct differentiation between unhappy marriages from ones that consist of physical, sexual, or emotional abuse.

You may be reading this passage and thinking, *But I prayed, and I sought the Lord diligently before saying "I do."* I can assure you I did the same. But I've since learned the difficulty of praying for guidance concerning something that you really want. This is where the enemy plays his infamous dance of confusion and deception in one's heart. He is skilled at taking the matters of the heart, where our deepest desires reside, and offering a counterfeit. It is my prayer that as you are holding this book in your hands, you would refuse the enemy's counterfeits to your soul hunger and receive the same lifesavers of practical coping strategies that Jesus provided to me. They are practical steps to God's healing plan.

I credit God's healing plan to where I am today, no longer suffering but writing to other sufferers. Please feel free to use whatever you feel will benefit you on your road to recovery. These steps are not presented in any order, except for the very first step. The first step is crucial. Setting a boundary was the beginning point for me. Boundaries are necessary for protecting the work of the Holy Spirit in our lives. Let me explain further.

Step 1: Setting boundaries

As a therapist, I am committed to teaching boundaries. In the Christian realm, boundaries are considered negative or even ungodly. But reading back over chapter 7 and Psalm 101:7, God, Himself, set boundaries: "No one who practices deceit will dwell in my house; no one who speaks falsely will stand in my presence." Clearly, we see God is determining who dwells in his house and who can stand in His presence, and the boundary is set against those who practice deceit and speaks falsely. If boundaries are good enough for God, then they are good enough for us. The first order of recovery for me included setting a boundary of marital separation to begin the healing process in my life. You may also find it necessary to remove yourself from the destructiveness of your relationship long enough to gain perspective and clarity.

Sharon Adler shares the following list of reasons people don't set healthy boundaries:

- Fear of what others think
- Assuming others will be mad
- Thinking it's not that important
- Not wanting the hassle
- Wanting to avoid conflict
- Preferring to go with the flow
- Fear of being seen as selfish or unforgiving fear of being alone[14]

Whatever your fear, please allow the Holy Spirit of our living God to direct your footsteps as He did mine. Believe it or not, God cares about emotional abuse in marriage. The church may not be ready to deal with it, but God has already set forth in His word that "oppression" of any kind is ungodly and unacceptable. Proverbs 18:14 says, "Who can bear a crushed spirit?" Psalm 32:8 says, *"I will instruct you and teach you in the way you should go; I will guide you with My eye."*

Step 2: Creating sacred space—Making room for God

Once a boundary is set and you have removed yourself from the chaos and toxicity, it is important to create a sacred space for you and the Lord that gives Him easy access to your heart and soul. Preferably, this is somewhere in your home. I took the liberty of redesigning my backyard patio that faces a calming lake. I purchased big green, leafy plants with orange, red, and yellow blossoms to provide an atmosphere of nature. These plants are placed strategically around my patio. I purchased new patio furniture that included plush, cushy, rocking, and swivel chairs to lull me into a comfortable mood as I listen to the sounds of flowing water from my outdoor cascading marble water fountain. I keep a good supply of devotional books, my journal, and the Bible handy to capture my long morning quiet talks with Jesus. I can tell you that I would not have made it had I not created the sacred space for communion with the Healer who understood my pain and sympathized with my weaknesses. This step reminded me of Zacchaeus of Luke 19:9 where he heard these words from Jesus: "Today, salvation has come to this house."

Step 3: External and internal changes

The loneliest time for any person separated from a spouse is bedtime. The empty bed can be cold and uninviting. To create a more inviting external atmosphere, I redecorated the master bedroom. I contracted a painter to paint the walls pink and gray. I found the most luscious pink swag rugs and pink lace curtains with matching wall-art accessories that made for a soft transition from a master bedroom to a misses bedroom. It was so much fun! It was also exhilarating as it invited new memories and experiences to the room. The full-body massage chair was an excellent addition to the room as well. All the external alterations to the room created brand-new internal changes in my mood. So try it. Look around your home and begin somewhere to create your sacred space. Any small changes you can make will give you a different and more pleasurable perception. I encourage you, my sister, to embrace the new thing that God may be doing in your life. Our external wilderness experiences can become our internal streams of water as we allow the Holy Spirit to transform our hurt and pain (Isaiah 43:19).

Step 4: Mind and body connection (Expand on mind body connection/mental health)

Please remember that the mind and body are intimately and intricately connected. The Lord led me to get creative with my spare time. I purchased an easel and a collective supply of art materials (i.e., paintbrushes, canvasses, water, and oil paints). For the first time, I allowed for the creative expression of my emotions. There was something very healing about creating colorful images of my emotional state that eliminated the need to hold onto negativity. Self-care took on an entire new meaning for me during this time. I changed my diet to include more fruits and vegetables, drank lemon water, and increased exercise regimes. I must admit, I still struggle with maintaining a good exercise regime. Initially, I found it difficult to achieve quality sleep. Until I began taking a few deep breaths, playing the Bible story app or listening to a book on audible until sleep became as natural as it had before. Third John 1:2 sums up this step beautifully, *"Beloved, I pray that you may prosper in all things and be in health, just as our soul prospers."*

Step 5: Word of God

I was led to many different online women's ministry sites and topical Bible studies that were used to bring the emotional support I desperately needed. Some of the websites and Bible studies are referenced in this book—*It Is Not Supposed to Be This Way* by Lysa Terkeurst, *The Emotionally Destructive Marriage* by Leslie Vernick, and *The Narcissistic Abuse Recovery Bible* by Shannon L. Adler. This emotional and mental support was most helpful. This provided me with a proper biblical view of broken marriages without the guilt and shame of people with little understanding and insight into this dynamic. But best of all was my quiet devotional time with the Lord where He would speak directly to me through Scripture daily. The outcome of these talks with Jesus was shared throughout this book. However, I am still in possession of what I entitled "Healing Notes," which is my personal journal that records every facet of my healing.

Biblical journaling is an exciting way to engage with the God of the Scripture and transform the way you interact with Him. Keeping a record of the spiritual insights on my journey will be something to share in my counseling ministry in my practice and with my church family. If you do not have a journal, I strongly recommend that you purchase one immediately. This will be one of your most precious possessions. The Lord instructed Jeremiah in chapter 30 verse 2, "*Thus says the Lord, the God of Israel: Write in a book all the words that I have spoken to you.*"

Step 6: Soul Sister Circle

The boundaries, internal and external changes provided through sacred spaces, prayer, Scripture, and physical self-care were enhanced as I created a small group of three sisters with whom I was grateful to share my journey. For the sake of privacy, I will not reveal these women, but the three of them know exactly who they are. One of the blessings of this group of soul sisters is that we were all experiencing the breakdown of our marriages at the same time, and because of that, we did not feel so alone. This Soul Sister Circle was a nonjudgmental, loving, and caring zone to share painful thoughts, emotions, experiences, memories, and, yes, sometimes tears as we underwent nasty legal entanglements. It is my prayer that you would also find such a group of sisters. Nothing ties hearts together tighter than familiarity in suffering. Scripture encourages us to "*bear one another's burdens and so fulfill the law of Christ*" (Galatians 6:2).

Step 7: Making radical adjustments

My clinical mentor spoken of in chapter 2 explains relationships this way. He says, "There are givers and takers. Takers take, and givers give. The problem is that takers have good pickers because they seem to always pick givers. However, givers have poor pickers evidenced by always picking takers." This sums up my entire relationship history. Because of this, I was forced to take a hard look at my picker and make some radical adjustments. I do not know your relationship history. But perhaps you could benefit from some of the radical adjustments I had to make outlined below:

1. *Have a list of deal-breakers.* If you do not determine what you will stand for, you will fall for anyone with the right words and wrong intentions. Please make sure you can articulate characteristics of a healthy relationship (see exhibit B for details), and better yet, be sure to commit to consistency and avoid rationalizations when vetting marriage material. As women, we are quick to rationalize unhealthy behaviors. We explain away ungodly behavior in favor of giving grace. Grace, as we mentioned earlier, is not designed to be a license to accept mistreatment. I term this "abusive grace." The Bible tells us that grace is a gift from God not to be haphazardly applied to cover up sin. As Christians, whether husbands or wives, we no longer live under the power of sin, but Christ died that we might belong to Him and live under His power over sin (see the discord in Romans 6:1–11).

2. *Falling for a man's potential.* Remember my brother who joked about the high hopes I had for the men in my life (see chapter 2). He may have been joking, but there was a strong undercurrent of truth in his joke. Falling in love with the projected good we see in people is a setup for a takedown. Before long, if you are not careful, you will be married to a "shadow" of a husband. I ran across a saying some time ago, and I think it is a good idea to share it here. It reads, "Sisters, when a man shows you who he is, believe him." The spiritual discernment we receive by walking with God will help us make a proper discovery and guide us toward proper action. Corrie Ten Boom's quote is applicable here. She says, "Discernment is God's call to intercession never to faultfinding." Hebrews 4:12 speaks of the alertness of truth to judge the thoughts and attitudes of the heart.

3. *Know when it is time to run.* Hanging on too long is when the relationship has caused you emotional, mental, and spiritual damage. Too long is when your dignity and self-respect are locked away in a closet, never to see the light of day again (see part 3 above "Gift of Goodbye"). You will know when it has gone too far when the sad days grow darker, and the bright days grow dimmer. Sometimes, you cannot even recognize the difference between the two. However, here are some clues to help distinguish the days. Keep an eye on your thoughts (irritability, hopelessness, helplessness), emotions (sad, anxious), and body sensations (tensed, neck/back pain), all of which will tell the story. Please do not underestimate the effects of stress. Stress is highly correlated to the risk of cardiovascular disease.[15] Recognize the effect the relationship is having upon you and your walk with God. Listen in on the disagreements that continue to resurface and resurface without resolution. Perpetual problems may reveal a lack of empathy and personal responsibility that are telltale signs of an unhealthy relationship. Believe it or not, the Bible speaks of toxic relationships and its damage to everyone around it. Think of King Saul in 1 Samuel 18 and see the damage to himself, his family, and his kingdom because of his toxic behaviors. Here is a quick Bible study for you. Take some time to explore these Scriptures that appear to instruct us on how to deal with unhealthy relationships: 1 Corinthians 15:33, Proverbs 13:20, Psalm 1:1, Proverbs 6:27, 1 Corinthians 5:11, 1 John 4:1, Amos 3:3.

4. *Stop rescue missions.* You know the relationship is unhealthy when you are constantly in rescue mission mode. Another term for this is *enabling* or *codependency*. Let me share with you a very simple definition for *codependency*: "doing for others that they could and should be doing for themselves and excusing poor choices and behaviors of others." When we will not lovingly confront poor treatment, we are participating in the continuation of unacceptable harmful

behavior such as lying, cheating, and dishonesty. We must be courageous enough to let others know when they are harming us and others. Pray for this courage. The Bible calls it speaking the truth in love (Ephesians 4:15). We are called to teach others how to treat us. Kindness is an ethical principle and a two-way street. My sisters, never excuse nor tolerate harmful behavior wherever it may be found. Refer to the chapter 7 discussion on "spiritual confrontation" confirmed by Galatians 6:1–2.

EXHIBIT B

Do Your Own Personal Work

Now that we have discussed God's healing plan and you have step-by-step instructions to guide your healing process, let's review ways to never find ourselves again in such a dire strait as a toxic marriage. Experience should be the best teacher, but there is the opportunity for Christian counseling to discover the root of relationship issues as I shared in my personal story in chapter 4. There is no shame to acknowledge your own weaknesses and contributions to the breakdown of a relationship. It would be foolish not to do so. Second Peter 2:22 warns us, "A dog returns to its vomit…and a sow that is washed returns to her wallowing in the mud." God forbid that we would continue to repeat patterns after patterns when the Lord stands ready to guide us with His eye upon us (Psalm 25).

Even after you have done your personal work, you may need a tool to help you evaluate future relationships. The below relationship questionnaire created by Leslie Vernick, PhD, is very helpful. See attached.

ARE YOU IN AN EMOTIONALLY DESTRUCTIVE RELATIONSHIP?

Leslie Vernick

From chapter 1, *The Emotionally Destructive Relationship: Seeing It! Stopping It! Surviving It!* (Harvest House Publishers, 2007)

Complete this questionnaire once for each relationship you are concerned about. For example, if you're evaluating your relationship with your spouse, answer each question about your spouse first. Don't combine answers about your spouse with answers about another relationship. You can apply the questionnaire to each of your relationships. It will help you not only identify whether your relationships are destructive but in what way they are destructive.

1. Does the person use physical force or threats of force to make you do something you don't want to do or to keep you from doing something you want to do?

    Never   Seldom   Sometimes   Frequently   Almost Always

2. Does the person use verbal weapons such as cursing, name calling, degrading comments, constant criticism, or blaming to get you to do something you don't want to do or to keep you from doing something you want to do?

Never   Seldom   Sometimes   Frequently   Almost Always

3. Does the person curse at you, call you names, humiliate you in public, or degrade you when he or she is unhappy with something you do?

Never   Seldom   Sometimes   Frequently   Almost Always

4. Does the person force or manipulate you to perform sexually in ways you do not want to?

Never   Seldom   Sometimes   Frequently   Almost Always

5. Do you ever feel afraid of the person?

Never   Seldom   Sometimes   Frequently   Almost Always

6. Does the person yell, scream, curse, or hurt you physically when he or she is frustrated or angry?

Never   Seldom   Sometimes   Frequently   Almost Always

7. Does the person threaten to alienate your children from you or use them to intimidate you into giving in to what he or she wants?

Never   Seldom   Sometimes   Frequently   Almost Always

8. Are you afraid to disagree with the person?

Never   Seldom   Sometimes   Frequently   Almost Always

9. When you share your thoughts and feelings about something important to you, does the person ignore you, make fun of you, or dismiss you?

Never   Seldom   Sometimes   Frequently   Almost Always

10. Are you verbally and/or physically abusive toward the person?

Never   Seldom   Sometimes   Frequently   Almost Always

11. Does the person always think he or she is right to the point of arguing with you until you concede or give up?

Never   Seldom   Sometimes   Frequently   Almost Always

12. Does the person make most of your decisions for you?

Never   Seldom   Sometimes   Frequently   Almost Always

13. Does the person control the family money, giving you little or no say?

Never   Seldom   Sometimes   Frequently   Almost Always

14. Have you given up things that were important to you because the person pressured you?

Never   Seldom   Sometimes   Frequently   Almost Always

15. Does the person pout or withdraw from you for extended periods of time when he or she is angry or upset with you?

Never   Seldom   Sometimes   Frequently   Almost Always

16. When you ask for a time out or don't want to talk about something anymore, does the person keep badgering you to engage?

Never   Seldom   Sometimes   Frequently   Almost Always

17. Does the person lie to you?

    Never   Seldom   Sometimes   Frequently   Almost Always

18. Have you observed the person lying to others?

    Never   Seldom   Sometimes   Frequently   Almost Always

19. Does the person tell you something didn't happen when you know it did?

    Never   Seldom   Sometimes   Frequently   Almost Always

20. Does the person question or challenge your certainty of what he or she said or did?

    Never   Seldom   Sometimes   Frequently   Almost Always

21. Does the person depend on you to meet all his or her needs?

    Never   Seldom   Sometimes   Frequently   Almost Always

22. Do you feel more like a child than an adult in the relationship?

    Never   Seldom   Sometimes   Frequently   Almost Always

23. Are you emotionally devastated when the person is upset with you or doesn't want to be in relationship with you?

    Never   Seldom   Sometimes   Frequently   Almost Always

24. When you try to talk with the person about your feelings or something that's bothering you, do you end up feeling like the trouble is entirely your fault?

Never   Seldom   Sometimes   Frequently   Almost Always

25. When the person does something wrong, does he or she blame you or anyone else for it?

Never   Seldom   Sometimes   Frequently   Almost Always

26. Does the other person make excuses for his or her behavior (anger, jealousy, lies)?

Never   Seldom   Sometimes   Frequently   Almost Always

27. Do you feel loved and cared for in the relationship?

Never   Seldom   Sometimes   Frequently   Almost Always

28. Can you safely express an opinion that is different from the person's?

Never   Seldom   Sometimes   Frequently   Almost Always

29. Does the person show interest in you and your needs?

Never   Seldom   Sometimes   Frequently   Almost Always

30. Are you able to express your honest thoughts and feelings with the person?

Never   Seldom   Sometimes   Frequently   Almost Always

31. When the person does something wrong, does he or she admit it and take responsibility for it?

Never   Seldom   Sometimes   Frequently   Almost Always

If you answered any question up through question 25 with anything other than never, you are likely in an unhealthy relationship. If you answered most questions with sometimes, frequently, and/or almost always, you are definitely in a destructive and likely an abusive relationship. Now go back and look at which questions in particular you answered with any answer other than never.

Questions 1–16 describe the main characteristics of an abusive relationship where the abuser's desire for power and control is at the root. If answering this questionnaire has revealed to you that you are in an abusive relationship, please seek appropriate help from those in your church or community who are experts in helping victims of abusive relationships. You will find information about various resources in Appendix 2. If you answered seldom to any question in this group, you still may be in danger, depending upon the severity of the abuse. Once a year is seldom, but it is still too often in a long-term relationship such as a marriage.

Question 10 looks in particular for patterns of mutual abuse. If you answered this question with frequently or almost always, then your relationship might be more mutually abusive. Review questions 1–16 and ask them about yourself. Are you engaging in the same abusive behaviors that you cite in the other person?

Questions 11–17 reflect less obvious ways in which the relationship may be controlling. That does not mean it is not abusive, but if you answered never to questions 1–9, you may be in a controlling relationship that is not obviously abusive.

Questions 17–20 describe a relationship where deceit is present. If most of your answers reflect problems in this area, your relationship is built on lies and it is unstable. You cannot trust someone who does not tell you the truth. Without trust, no relationship can endure.

Questions 21–23 describe a relationship that is overdependent.

Questions 24–26 describe a person who does not take personal responsibility for behavior or wrongdoing.

Stop here and name some of the specific destructive elements in your relationship with this particular person. Is there physical, verbal or sexual abuse? How about controlling behaviors and attitudes? Is there more mutual abuse? Are you too dependent? Is there deceit or a lack of personal accountability or responsibility?

Questions 27–31 describe the basic elements of a healthy relationship. If you answered never or seldom to any of these questions, your answers indicate that your relationship is unhealthy and probably destructive.

Right now you may feel overwhelmed and frightened. These feelings are normal for anyone facing difficult truths. If you want to become healthier and have better relationships, I want to assure you that you can begin working on your part.

I don't want to scare you, but it's important that you understand the serious consequences of destructive relationships so that you will do all you can to change these patterns. I know, it feels easier to simply close your eyes or try to get by, hoping that the damage won't be too bad, but trust me: ignoring destruction doesn't ever make it better or even neutral. The damage only grows.[16]

EXHIBIT C

How Can the Church Help?

There is something to be said about a wounded healer. It is someone who has been wounded but willing to walk with others struggling with the same wounds. Organizations such as Alcohol Anonymous and Narcotic Anonymous have been successful in this endeavor. I have often wondered why the church does not take a similar approach to helping its own. I am an addictions professional and have worked with those caught in addiction for many years. I have noticed the applicable nature of these 12-step programs as ancillary to professional counseling. Many have been delivered through these types of programs where wounded healers lead the way from personal experience and recovery expertise.

Meet Steve—A wounded healer

It was the early nineties, and a young man named Steve Grissom was looking for help. He was divorced, and he needed support and advice from people who truly understood just how hard it was to go through divorce. He couldn't find exactly what he needed. So Steve researched all he could about divorce-related topics, took notes, and started leading an informal support group program himself. He began each session by teaching on a topic related to separation and divorce and occasionally showed a video. He and his new wife, Cheryl (who had also been through a divorce), would then lead the group in a discussion of that topic. The format worked well, and the group members found it helpful. But it was a lot of work, and Steve didn't really feel qualified for the role. He started thinking, *Someone needs to create a divorce ministry tool for people like me.* It turns out—that somebody was Steve.

Today, DivorceCare is a thirteen-week, video-based program designed to minister to those suffering from the pain of separation or divorce. This program creates a safe place for church members to find the support needed to manage the emotional roller coaster of broken families and learn practice tools for recovering from such experiences. Every church should offer such a program. Here people will find "understanding and acceptance, encouragement and hope, good advice and a structured approach" to healing. The program covers topics such as grief, anger, depression, loneliness, fear, anxiety, financial, and legal assistance, all of which the church fails to address when there is a divorce or separation among its congregation. What is the harm of releasing judgment long enough to offer support? Chapters 6, 7, and 8 gives several examples of the unintended collateral pain caused by ill-advised and uninformed congregates that, in many instances, can cause secondary trauma to this population of church members. I would never want anyone to experience the advice I received at church that I shared in chapter 6, 7, and 8 ever again.

The wonderful thing about DivorceCare, if your church is not able to actually offer the group meetings, the pastor or leadership should be aware that referral to churches offering the group is equally effectives. DivorceCare even offer daily encouraging emails with emotional tips and further reference material. Finding a DivorceCare group is easy as a quick online search at www.divorcecare.org and find a group closest to your area. DivorceCare offers training and assistance to start a group in your church. The only qualification for leadership is that you have experienced divorce yourself. It is a Christ-centered, Scripture-driven program. I highly recommend this program from personal and professional experience.

DISCUSSION QUESTIONS

Take some time to review some of the major quotes and discussion questions from the book *The End of Forever*. You may meditate upon the author's lessons learned and spiritual shifts to incorporate insights into your own life. In a group format, you may discuss the questions or quietly contemplate them during individual devotional time with the Lord.

PART I
INTRODUCTION

1. Do you agree with the author's opinion? "Efforts to deny the damage of divorce in the church are still alive today and are responsible for short-circuiting the healing of God's people on every level. But even more damaging is the church's response to its divorced members."

2. Read the author's note again, and determine if she accomplished her mission to reveal the love of Christ in His Word to lead you through one of the most painful experiences in life—divorce/separation.

PART II
THE BEGINNING OF FOREVER

Chapter 1
God's Ideal vs. Satan's Raw Deal

1. Do you identify with the special purpose and nature God created you with?

2. How are you tolerating your broken relationship?

3. Can you identify with the author's description, "the two that became one flesh are now two flesh-torn individuals"?

Chapter 2
Emotional Paralysis

1. The author makes the consistent point to share her desire for her marriage to be one that would "glorify God in life-long service," and she also desired that the "love of God would be the blueprint" for her husband's love for her. Can you relate to this, or does it seem a bit overreaching?

2. Have you ever experienced "emotional paralysis" and the "Double D" as you encountered the experience of divorce or separation?

3. Has Leah's lesson encouraged you to focus upon praising God with your life even with the inattentiveness of your husband?

Lesson learned
Power of compassion

I have learned to ask God for the love and compassion to see my husband in a different way. Acknowledging his woundedness that blinds him to his own sinful behavior, this view of him empowers me to forgive even though reconciliation may be impossible. This view enables me to leave him in God's hands and not mine.

Spiritual shift
Forgive and live

True forgiveness does not always mean reconciliation but is required for the spiritual restoration of my soul. Initially, forgiveness is a choice then a long-term process that prevents the enemy from filling my heart with hatred and bitterness.

I truly released myself when I entered the arena of forgiveness. Forgiveness is the good fight of faith that promises good soldiers the crown of life (2 Timothy 2:3 and James 1:12).

PART III
THE THREAT OF FOREVER

Chapter 3
Losing a Dream but Waking Up to Reality

1. What is your understanding of the author's deduction that "Harsh and toxic circumstances may lead to separating from our man but never our God. Yes, sometimes, the gift of goodbye is compulsory"?

2. The author acknowledges the ambivalence of trusting God in times of devasting experiences and shares the comfort she received from the story of the Samaritan woman. Can you find comfort from the way Jesus met this woman at her deepest point of pain?

3. What dreams are you holding onto that are difficult to let go of?

Lesson learned
Learning who is leading in times of trouble

God often leads His people through the wilderness to get to the promised land (Exodus 14–16). God does not cause the wilderness experience. He is leading us through the wilderness of brokenness, barrenness, and emptiness of destructive marriages. I learned to look for the lessons in the wilderness. They will be important to take into the promised land.

Spiritual shift
Handling wilderness moments

Learning to take comfort in the middle ground between the wilderness and the promised land, sometimes, the blessings are found in the pain we must walk through because this is where we meet Jesus and find Him to be intently at work preparing our souls for heaven.

Bread will fall from heaven to feed us during times of famine in our lives here on earth. Exodus 16:35 is proof of God's provision and deliverance during our wilderness moments. Let us burst out into song with Moses: *The Lord is my strength and song, and He has become my salvation; He is my God and I will praise Him; The Lord is a man of war; the Lord is His name* (Exodus 15:2, 3).

Chapter 4
Searching for Love in Human Hearts

1. Were you able to identify with the author's personal story in any way? What is your understanding of the "gift of goodbye"?

2. Have you truly explored any childhood issues that may have inadvertently left you exposed to toxicity in romantic relationships?

3. Share or journal some of your experiences searching for love in human hearts.

Lesson learned

Move away from men (or people in general) that will take pleasure in receiving more than they are willing to provide.

Spiritual shift

It is important to explore childhood events that may be blinding us from current issues in life. For me, it was a well-established habit of ignoring the bad behavior of men in my life. Jesus does not ignore bad behavior. It cost Him His life.

The cross is a symbol that sin cannot be excused, overlooked, or ignored in my life, your life, or that of others. I now understand this principle and am able to allow my father to rest in peace and appropriately grieve the loss of my marriage so that I can also rest in peace.

PART IV
SHAME OF FOREVER

Chapter 5
Broken Vows

1. Do you agree with the author's assertion that the most signif-icant infirmity of divorce is the attached stigma of "shame"?

2. Can your story of divorce be retold with the grace and courage that the Lord taught the author?

3. What is your understanding of a "necessary separation"?

Lesson learned

For sharing this lesson learned, I will use the words of Leslie Vernick: "Healing a destructive marriage can never be the sole responsibility of one person in the relationship. It always takes two people willing to work to achieve godly change."[17]

Leslie Vernick is a Christian counselor and author who is gifted with spiritual discernment to share biblical truth about toxicity in marriage from a sensitive, practical yet responsible perspective.

Spiritual shift

In a marriage, both have a spiritual responsibility to God and one another. However, that responsibility is not a license to subjugate per-sonal accountability to accept sinful behavior. I am learning to refuse to relinquish my spiritual responsibility to hold my spouse accountable for sinful behavior. It serves no one to allow sin to go unnoticed.

PART V
THE END OF FOREVER

Chapter 6
"Great Is Your Faithfulness"

1. What are your thoughts about the author's declarations? "The end of forever was the beginning of never. Never again would I offer myself on the altar of broken vows. Never again would I accept a dream that was not hand-picked by God Himself."

2. Which of the author's life verses do you resonate with the most?

3. Share or journal some of the unhelpful, "cookie-cutter" responses you have received from others in their attempt to comfort you.

Lesson learned

There are no cookie-cutter marriages, so then how can there be cookie-cutter responses to all marriage problems? You cannot take the same paintbrush to color all marriages. The amazing thing I learned in this journey is that the love of Christ and His Word are extremely relevant, revolutionary, and redemptive to all His children and every problem they face. My life verses are proof of this.

Spiritual shift

Live wholeheartedly for Jesus as a protective measure against the snares of Satan.

PART VI
THE HOPE OF FOREVER

Chapter 7
Misuse of Scripture

1. The author believes suffering has gone too far when we allow destructive behaviors to exist without healthy boundaries. She states that "even God calls for healthy boundaries." Read Psalm 101:7, and discuss whether you believe God sets boundaries.

2. Discuss whether you believe grace should cover serious and painful behavior of others, especially a spouse.

3. Do you agree with the author's opinion that "Grace is not misrepresented in Scripture; it is misapplied by the people of Scripture"?

Lesson learned

It is easy to misuse Scripture by reading into it what we already believe. Rather, we want to allow Scripture to be our belief system (2 Timothy 2:15).

Spiritual shift

To appropriately apply grace with spiritual discernment requires I talk to Jesus before opening my mouth to others. I am instructed to remember that here on earth, I only see dimly, and my own understanding can be darkened by my own pride and prejudices (Proverbs 3:5–6).

Chapter 8
The Church's Response

1. What are your thoughts of the "spiritual discernment" and the need for the church to offer comfort and compassion rather than advice when dealing with issues of divorce?

2. How comforting was the family prayer offered by the author?

3. Do you agree with divorce as one of the most profound crises of faith?

Lesson learned

There is a way that seems right to a man, but the end thereof leads to destruction (Proverbs 14:12). Opinions are just opinions and should be repudiated by God's Word.

Spiritual shift

Prayer changes everything, and everything is changed by prayer. The prayer approach will relinquish the pride and presumptive pronouncements of blame and shame.

Chapter 9
Delightful Detours

1. Has your wrong turns of divorce and separation led to God's U-turns in your life?

2. Do you agree with the author's advice to churches to follow SMART goals when ministering to the divorced or separated?

3. What missed opportunities can you turn into ministry?

Lesson learned

I am learning to see delightful detours as routes to overcome life's disappointments. Interestingly though, the idea that a failed marriage is a delightful detour is equally intriguing as the notion that there is an end of forever. What detours are you facing today, and what routes do you need to correct to find the hope and comfort of God?

Spiritual shift

Moving from worry to worship in the face of disappointments forces us to search deeper for the faithfulness of God. I have no shame in sharing with you that this particular spiritual shift for me has been most difficult to make.

There are still days that my fight with fear wins the battle but not the war. Like David, let us daily open windows wide to offer prayer, praise, and thanksgiving to a hearing and very-present God.

PART VII
THE ETERNAL FOREVER

1. What necessary preparation do you need to make yourself ready for the return of the heavenly Bridegroom?

2. Share your thoughts about the author's ability to redeem her dream with Revelations 19:7, 8.

3. Has this journey of healing and restoration empowered you to believe in your true value to God and His kingdom as you await His return?

4. Are you looking forward to the eternal marriage where you will enjoy intimate and everlasting fellowship with Jesus Christ, the heavenly Bridegroom—where forever will never end?

FINAL TAKEAWAY MEDITATIONS

1. How has Ellen G. White's advice in the various letters to hurting women in troubling marriages ministered to your heart as you read her guidance throughout the book?

2. Did you find the promised encouragement, education, and empowerment in the restorative healing of Christ as you received the therapeutic lessons and made the spiritual shifts shared throughout the book?

3. Are you leaving this book with the recognition that you are still valuable to the kingdom of God even after divorce?

ENDNOTES

1   https://marriedpeoplechurches.org/author/barna/.
2   Finke, Roger; Rodney Stark (2005). The Churching of America, 1776–2005. Rutgers University Press. pp. 22–23. ISBN 0-8135-3553-0. online at Google Books.
3   https://m.egwwritings.org/en/book/122.360.
4   Alder, Shannon L. The Narcissistic Abuse Recovery Bible: Spiritual Recovery from Narcissistic and Emotional Abuse. Cedar Fort, Inc. 2018. (p. 42).
5   TerKeurst, Lysa. *Uninvited.* Thomas Nelson. 2016. (p. 14).
6   B Three Toxic Effects of Shame We Can Overcome | Chase Oaks. https://www.chaseoaks.org/blog/three-toxic-effects-of-shame-we-can-overcome.
7   Vernick, Leslie. The Emotionally Destructive Marriage. The Crown Publishing Group. 2013. p. 194.
8   Jose, Stephanie. Progressing through Grief. Althea Press. 2016. P. 21.
9   Ellen G. White Estate: Daily Devotional—Lift Him Up. https://whiteestate.org/devotional/lhu/09_17/.
10   Letter 34, 1890. TSB 77.1—TSB entitled "Separation rather than Apostacy."
11   https://www.thegospelcoalition.org/article/hard-conversation/.
12   Autumn Leaves (NZ) Limited: Divorce and Remarriage. https://autumnleaves.co.nz/newsletters/editorials/divorce-and-remarriage/.
13   The Adventist Home—Ellen G. White Writings. https://m.egwwritings.org/en/book/128.1556.
14   Alder, Shannon L., *The Narcissistic Abuse Recovery Bible: Spiritual Recovery from Narcissistic and Emotional Abuse* (Cedar Fort Inc.), 145.
15   Steptoe A and Kivimäki M. Stress and cardiovascular disease. Nat Rev Cardiol. April 3, 2012; 9(6):360-70. doi: 10.1038/nrcardio.2012.45. PMID: 22473079
16   Leslie Vernick, *The Emotionally Destructive Marriage* (The Crown Publishing Group, 2013).
17   Vernick, Leslie. The Emotionally Destructive Marriage. The Crown Publishing Group. 2013. p. 194.

—❧ ❧—

ABOUT THE AUTHOR

Phyllis McColister, MS, LMHC, CAP, received her master's degree in mental health counseling from Palm Beach Atlantic University and a bachelor's degree in psychology from Barry University. She is licensed by the state of Florida as a licensed mental health counselor and a qualified clinical supervisor. She is also certified as an addictions professional with the Florida Certification Board.

Phyllis is the founder and CEO of Healing Waters Counseling—a private practice in Fort Pierce, Florida. She also works as an adjunct professor at Indian River State College in the Human Services Department in Fort Pierce, Florida.

In all her academic and professional accolades, Phyllis is known for her love and support of hurting people in general and women in particular. Her faith drives her values and ethics that has led to Christian counseling, speaking, Bible study teaching, and prayer ministering with the Seventh-Day Adventist Church.

Phyllis is a firm believer in empowering individuals and families in managing a myriad of emotional, mental, and spiritual dynamics often associated with overcoming substance abuse and co-occurring mental health problems.

She is highly skilled in working with hospice patients and helping clients recover from trauma-related experiences. Phyllis has lived in the St. Lucie County community of Florida for over seventeen years. She enjoys many strong relationships in the mental health community, juvenile justice system, state health and human service agencies, and local school systems.

Phyllis takes great pleasure in presenting public mental health seminars, stress management support groups, and interpersonal skills training. Phyllis is a highly regarded clinician, speaker, and recently published author.